Notes From Lectures And Discourses

by

Swami Vivekananda

Notes From Lectures And Discourses
by Swami Vivekananda

ISBN: 978-93-59393-71-1

Published by

DOUBLE 9 BOOKS

2/13-B, Ansari Road
Daryaganj, New Delhi – 110002
info@double9books.com
www.double9books.com
Tel. 011-40042856

ABOUT THE AUTHOR

Swami Vivekananda was born Narendranath Datta in India on January 12, 1863. He died on July 4, 1902, and was the most important student of the Indian saint Ramakrishna. He was an important part of bringing Vedanta and Yoga to the West. He is also charged with making people more aware of other religions and making Hinduism a major world religion. Vivekananda had a lot of success at the Parliament. In the years that followed, he gave hundreds of lectures across the United States, England, and Europe to spread the main ideas of Hinduism. He also started the Vedanta Society of New York and the Vedanta Society of San Francisco, which is now the Vedanta Society of Northern California. Both of these groups became the basis for Vedanta Societies in the West. Vivekananda was one of the most important philosophers and social reformers in India at the time. He was also one of the most successful and powerful Vedanta missionaries in the West.People now think of him as one of the most important people in modern India and Hinduism. Mahatma Gandhi said that after reading Vivekananda's works, he loved his country a thousand times more.

CONTENTS

On Karma-Yoga

Isolation of the soul from all objects, mental and physical, is the goal; when that is attained, the soul will find that it was alone all the time, and it required no one to make it happy. As long as we require someone else to make us happy, we are slaves. When the Purusha finds that It is free, and does not require anything to complete Itself, that this nature is quite unnecessary, then freedom (Kaivalya) is attained.

Men run after a few dollars and do not think anything of cheating a fellow-being to get those dollars; but if they would restrain themselves, in a few years they would develop such characters as would bring them millions of dollars — if they wanted them. Then their will would govern the universe. But we are all such fools!

What is the use of talking of one's mistakes to the world? They cannot thereby be undone. For what one has done one must suffer; one must try and do better. The world sympathises only with the strong and the powerful.

It is only work that is done as a free-will offering to humanity and to nature that does not bring with it any binding attachment.

Duty of any kind is not to be slighted. A man who does the lower work is not, for that reason only, a lower man than he who does the higher work; a man should not be judged by the nature of his duties, but by the manner in which he does them. His manner of doing them and his power to do them are indeed the test of a man. A shoemaker who can turn out a strong, nice pair of shoes in the shortest possible time is a better man, according to his profession and his work, than a professor who talks nonsense every day of his life.

Every duty is holy, and devotion to duty is the highest form of the worship of God; it is certainly a source of great help in enlightening and emancipating the deluded and ignorance-encumbered souls of the Baddhas — the bound ones.

By doing well the duty which is nearest to us, the duty which is in our hands now, we make ourselves stronger and improving our strength in this manner step by step, we may even reach a state in which it shall be our privilege to do the most coveted and honoured duties in life and in society.

Nature's justice is uniformly stern and unrelenting.

The most practical man would call life neither good nor evil.

Every successful man must have behind him somewhere tremendous integrity, tremendous sincerity, and that is the cause of his signal success in life. He may not have been perfectly unselfish; yet he was tending towards it. If he had been perfectly unselfish, his would have been as great a success as that of the Buddha or of the Christ. The degree of unselfishness marks the degree of success everywhere.

The great leaders of mankind belong to higher fields than the field of platform work.

However we may try, there cannot be any action which is perfectly pure or any which is perfectly impure, taking purity or impurity in the sense of injury or non-injury. We cannot breathe or live without injuring others, and every morsel of food we eat is taken from another's mouth; our very lives are crowding out some other lives. It may be those of men, or animals, or small fungi, but someone somewhere we have to crowd out. That being the case, it naturally follows that perfection can never be attained by work. We may work through all eternity, but there will be no way out of this intricate maze: we may work on and on and on, but there will be no end.

The man who works through freedom and love cares nothing for results. But the slave wants his whipping; the servant wants his pay. So with all life; take for instance the public life. The public speaker wants a little applause or a little hissing and hooting. If you keep him in a corner without it, you kill him, for he requires it. This is working through slavery. To expect something in return, under such conditions, becomes second nature. Next comes the work of the servant, who requires some pay; I give this, and you give me that. Nothing is easier to say, "I work for work's sake", but nothing is so difficult to attain. I would go twenty miles on my hands and knees to look on the face of the man who can work for work's sake. There is a motive somewhere. If it is not money, it is power. If it is not power, it is gain. Somehow, somewhere, there is a motive power. You are my friend, and I want to work for you and with you. This is all very well, and every moment I may make protestation of my sincerity. But take care, you must be sure to agree with me! If you do not, I shall no longer take care of you or live for you! This kind of work for a motive brings misery. That work alone brings unattachment and bliss, wherein we work as masters of our own minds.

The great lesson to learn is that I am not the standard by which the whole universe is to be judged; each man is to be judged by his own idea, each race by its own standard and ideal, each custom of each country by its own reasoning and conditions. American customs are the result of the environment in which the Americans live and Indian customs are the result of the environment in which the Indians are; and so of China, Japan, England, and every other country.

We all find ourselves in the position for which we are fit, each ball finds its own hole; and if one has some capacity above another, the world will find that out too, in this universal adjusting that goes on. So it is no use to grumble. There may be a rich man who is wicked, yet there must be in that man certain qualities that made him rich; and if any other man has the same qualities, he will also become rich. What is the use of fighting and complaining? That will not help us to better things. He who grumbles at the little thing that has fallen to his lot to do will grumble at everything. Always grumbling, he will lead a miserable life, and everything will be a failure. But that man who does his duty as he goes, putting, his shoulder to the wheel, will see the light, and higher and higher duties will fall to his share.

On Fanaticism

There are fanatics of various kinds. Some people are wine fanatics and cigar fanatics. Some think that if men gave up smoking cigars, the world would arrive at the millennium. Women are generally amongst these fanatics. There was a young lady here one day, in this class. She was one of a number of ladies in Chicago who have built a house where they take in the working people and give them music and gymnastics. One day this young lady was talking about the evils of the world and said she knew the remedy. I asked, "How do you know?" and she answered, "Have you seen Hull House?" In her opinion, this Hull House is the one panacea for all the evils that flesh is heir to. This will grow upon her. I am sorry for her. There are some fanatics in India who think that if a woman could marry again when her husband died, it would cure all evil. This is fanaticism.

When I was a boy I thought that fanaticism was a great element in work, but now, as I grow older, I find out that it is not.

There may be a woman who would steal and make no objection to taking someone else's bag and going away with it. But perhaps that woman does not smoke. She becomes a smoke fanatic, and as soon as she finds a man smoking, she strongly disapproves of him, because he smokes a cigar. There may be a man who goes about cheating people; there is no trusting him; no woman is safe with him. But perhaps this scoundrel does not drink wine. If so, he sees nothing good in anyone who drinks wine. All these wicked things that he himself does are of no consideration. This is only natural human selfishness and one-sidedness.

You must also remember that the world has God to govern it, and He has not left it to our charity. The Lord God is its Governor and Maintainer, and in spite of these wine fanatics and cigar fanatics, and all sorts of marriage fanatics, it would go on. If all these persons were to die, it would go on none the worse.

Do you not remember in your own history how the "Mayflower" people came out here, and began to call themselves Puritans? They were very pure and good as far as they went, until they began to persecute other people; and throughout the history of mankind it has been the same. Even those that run away from persecution indulge in persecuting others as soon as a favourable opportunity to do so occurs.

In ninety cases out of a hundred, fanatics must have bad livers, or they are dyspeptics, or are in some way diseased. By degrees even physicians will find out that fanaticism is a kind of disease. I have seen plenty of it. The Lord save me from it!

My experience comes to this, that it is rather wise to avoid all sorts of fanatical reforms. This world is slowly going on; let it go slowly. Why are you in a hurry? Sleep well and keep your nerves in good order; eat right food, and have sympathy with the world. Fanatics only make hatred. Do you mean to say that the temperance fanatic loves these poor people who become drunkards? A fanatic is a fanatic simply because he expects to get something for himself in return. As soon as the battle is over, he goes for the spoil. When you come out of the company of fanatics you may learn how really to love and sympathise. And the more you attain of love and sympathy, the less will be your power to condemn these poor creatures; rather you will sympathise with their faults. It will become possible for you to sympathise with the drunkard and to know that he is also a man like yourself. You will then try to understand the many circumstances that are dragging him down, and feel that if you had been in his place you would perhaps have committed suicide. I remember a woman whose husband was a great drunkard, and she complained to me of his becoming so. I replied, "Madam, if there were twenty millions of wives like yourself, all husbands would become drunkards." I am convinced that a large number of drunkards are manufactured by their wives. My business is to tell the truth and not to flatter anyone. These unruly women from whose minds the words *bear* and *forbear* are gone for ever, and whose false ideas of independence lead them to think that men should be at their feet, and who begin to howl as soon as men dare to say anything to them which they do not like — such women are becoming the bane of the world, and it is a wonder that they do not drive half the men in it to commit suicide. In this way things should not go on. Life is not so easy as they believe it to be; it is a more serious business!

A man must not only have faith but intellectual faith too. To make a man take up everything and believe it, would be to make him a lunatic. I once had a book sent me, which said I must believe everything told in it. It said there was no soul, but that there were gods and goddesses in heaven, and a thread of light going from each of our heads to heaven! How did the writer know all these things? She had been inspired, and wanted me to believe it too; and because I refused, she said, "You must be a very bad man; there is no hope for you!" This is fanaticism.

Work Is Worship

The highest man *cannot* work, for there is no binding element, no attachment, no ignorance in him. A ship is said to have passed over a mountain of magnet ore, and all the bolts and bars were drawn out, and it went to pieces. It is in ignorance that struggle remains, because we are all really atheists. Real theists cannot work. We are atheists more or less. We do not see God or believe in Him. He is G-O-D to us, and nothing more. There are moments when we think He is near, but then we fall down again. When you see Him, who struggles for whom? Help the Lord! There is a proverb in our language, "Shall we teach the Architect of the universe how to build?" So those are the highest of mankind who do not work. The next time you see these silly phrases about the world and how we must all help God and do this or that for Him, remember this. Do not think such thoughts; they are too selfish. All the work you do is subjective, is done for your own benefit. God has not fallen into a ditch for you and me to help Him out by building a hospital or something of that sort. He allows you to work. He *allows* you to exercise your muscles in this great gymnasium, not in order to help Him but that you may help yourself. Do you think even an ant will die for want of your help? Most arrant blasphemy! The world does not need you at all. The world goes on you are like a drop in the ocean. A leaf does not move, the wind does not blow without Him. Blessed are we that we are given the privilege of working for Him, not of helping Him. Cut out this word "help" from your mind. You cannot help; it is blaspheming. You are here yourself at His pleasure. Do you mean to say, you help Him? You worship. When you give a morsel of food to the dog, you worship the dog as God. God is in that dog. He is the dog. He is all and in all. We are allowed to worship Him. Stand in that reverent attitude to the whole universe, and then will come perfect non-attachment. This should be your duty. This is the proper attitude of work. This is the secret taught by Karma-Yoga.

Work Without Motive

At the forty-second meeting of the Ramakrishna Mission held at the premises No. 57 Râmkânta Bose Street, Baghbazar, Calcutta, on the 20th March, 1898, Swami Vivekananda gave an address on "Work without Motive", and spoke to the following effect:

When the Gita was first preached, there was then going on a great controversy between two sects. One party considered the Vedic Yajnas and animal sacrifices and such like Karmas to constitute the whole of religion. The other preached that the killing of numberless horses and cattle cannot be called religion. The people belonging to the latter party were mostly Sannyâsins and followers of Jnâna. They believed that the giving up of all work and the gaining of the knowledge of the Self was the only path to Moksha By the preaching of His great doctrine of work without motive, the Author of the Gita set at rest the disputes of these two antagonistic sects.

Many are of opinion that the Gita was not written at the time of the Mahâbhârata, but was subsequently added to it. This is not correct. The special teachings of the Gita are to be found in every part of the Mahabharata, and if the Gita is to be expunged, as forming no part of it, every other portion of it which embodies the same teachings should be similarly treated.

Now, what is the meaning of working without motive? Nowadays many understand it in the sense that one is to work in such a way that neither pleasure nor pain touches his mind. If this be its real meaning, then the animals might be said to work without motive. Some animals devour their own offspring, and they do not feel any pangs at all in doing so. Robbers ruin other people by robbing them of their possessions; but if they feel quite callous to pleasure or pain, then they also would be working without motive. If the meaning of it be such, then one who has a stony heart, the worst of criminals, might be considered to be working without motive. The walls have no feelings of pleasure or pain, neither has a stone, and it cannot be said that they are working without motive. In the above sense the doctrine is a potent instrument in the hands of the wicked. They would go on doing wicked deeds, and would pronounce themselves as working without a motive. If such be the significance of working without a motive, then a fearful doctrine has been put forth by the preaching of the Gita. Certainly this is not the meaning. Furthermore, if we look into the lives of those who were connected with the preaching of the Gita, we should find them living quite a different life. Arjuna killed Bhishma and Drona in battle, but withal, he sacrificed all his self-interest and desires and his lower self millions of times.

Gita teaches Karma-Yoga. We should work through Yoga (concentration). In such concentration in action (Karma-Yoga), there is no consciousness of the lower ego present. The consciousness that I am doing this and that is never present when one works through Yoga. The Western people do not understand this. They say that if there be no consciousness of ego, if this ego is gone, how then can a man work? But when one works with concentration, losing all consciousness of oneself the work that is done will be infinitely better, and this every one may have experienced in his own life. We perform many works subconsciously, such as the digestion of food etc., many others consciously, and others again by becoming immersed in Samâdhi as it were, when there is no consciousness of the smaller ego. If the painter, losing the consciousness of his ego, becomes completely immersed in his painting, he will be able to produce masterpieces. The good cook concentrates his whole self on the food-material he handles; he loses all other consciousness for the time being. But they are only able to do perfectly a single work in this way, to which they are habituated. The Gita teaches that all works should be done thus. He who is one with the Lord through Yoga performs all his works by becoming immersed in concentration, and does not seek any personal benefit. Such a performance of work brings only good to the world, no evil can come out of it. Those who work thus never do anything for themselves.

The result of every work is mixed with good and evil. There is no good work that has not a touch of evil in it. Like smoke round the fire, some evil always clings to work. We should engage in such works as bring the largest amount of good and the smallest measure of evil. Arjuna killed Bhishma and Drona; if this had not been done Duryodhana could not have been conquered, the force of evil would have triumphed over the force of good, and thus a great calamity would have fallen on the country. The government of the country would have been usurped by a body of proud unrighteous kings, to the great misfortune of the people. Similarly, Shri Krishna killed Kamsa, Jarâsandha, and others who were tyrants, but not a single one of his deeds was done for himself. Every one of them was for the good of others. We are reading the Gita by candle-light, but numbers of insects are being burnt to death. Thus it is seen that some evil clings to work. Those who work without any consciousness of their lower ego are not affected with evil, for they work for the good of the world. To work without motive, to work unattached, brings the highest bliss and freedom. This secret of Karma-Yoga is taught by the Lord Shri Krishna in the Gita.

Sadhanas Or Preparations For Higher Life

If atavism gains, you go down; if evolution gains, you go on. Therefore, we must not allow atavism to take place. Here, in my own body, is the first work of the study. We are too busy trying to mend the ways of our neighbours, that is the difficulty. We must begin with our own bodies. The heart, the liver, etc., are all atavistic; bring them back into consciousness, control them, so that they will obey your commands and act up to your wishes. There was a time when we had control of the liver; we could shake the whole skin, as can the cow. I have seen many people bring the control back by sheer hard practice. Once an impress is made, it is there. Bring back all the submerged activities — the vast ocean of action. This is the first part of the great study, and it is absolutely necessary for our social well-being. On the other hand, only the consciousness need not be studied all the time.

Then there is the other part of study, not so necessary in our social life, which tends to liberation. Its direct action is to free the soul, to take the torch into the gloom, to clean out what is behind, to shake it up or even defy it, and to make us march onward piercing the gloom. That is the goal — the superconscious. Then when that state is reached, this very man becomes divine, becomes free. And to the mind thus trained to transcend all, gradually this universe will begin to give up its secrets; the book of nature will be read chapter after chapter, till the goal is attained, and we pass from this valley of life and death to that One, where death and life do not exist, and we know the Real and become the Real.

The first thing necessary is a quiet and peaceable life. If I have to go about the world the whole day to make a living, it is hard for me to attain to anything very high in this life. Perhaps in another life I shall be born under more propitious circumstances. But if I am earnest enough, these very circumstances will change even in this birth. Was there anything you did not get which you really wanted? It could not be. For it is the want that creates the body. It is the light that has bored the holes, as it were, in your head, called the eyes. If the light had not existed, you would have had no eyes. It is sound that had made the ears. The object of perception existed first, before you made the organ. In a few hundred thousand years or earlier, we may have other organs to perceive electricity and other things. There is no desire for a peaceful mind. Desire will not come unless there is something outside to fulfil it. The outside something just bores a hole in the body, as it were, and tries to get into the mind. So, when the desire will arise to have a peaceful, quiet life, that *shall come* where everything shall be propitious for the development of the mind — you may take that as my experience. It may come after thousands of lives, but it must come. Hold on to that, the desire. You cannot have the strong desire if its object was not outside for you already. Of course you must understand, there is a difference between desire and desire. The master said, "My child, if you desire after God, God shall come to you." The disciple did not understand his master fully. One day both went to bathe in a river, and the master said, "Plunge in", and the boy did so. In a moment the master was upon him, holding him down. He would not let the boy come up. When the boy struggled and was exhausted, he let him go. "Yes, my child, how did you feel there;" "Oh, the desire for a breath of air!" "Do you have that kind of desire for God?" "No, sir." "Have that kind of desire for God and you shall have God."

That, without which we cannot live, must come to us. If it did not come to us, life could not go on.

If you want to be a Yogi, you must be free and place yourself in circumstances where you are alone and free from all anxiety. He who desires for a comfortable and nice life and at the same time wants to realise the Self is like the fool who, wanting to cross the river, caught hold of a crocodile mistaking it for a log of wood. "Seek ye first the Kingdom of God and His righteousness, and all these things shall be added unto you." Unto him everything who does not care for anything. Fortune is like a flirt; she cares not for him who wants her, but she is at the feet of him who does not care for her. Money comes and showers itself upon one who does not care for it; so does fame come in abundance until it is a trouble and a burden. They always come to the Master. The slave never gets anything. The Master is he who can live in spite of them, whose life does not depend upon the little, foolish things of the world. Live for an ideal, and that one ideal alone. Let it be so great, so strong, that there may be nothing else left in the mind; no place for anything else, no time for anything else.

How some people give all their energies, time, brain, body, and everything, to become rich! They have no time for breakfast! Early in the morning they are out and at work! They die in the attempt — ninety per cent of them — and the rest when they make money, cannot enjoy it. That is grand! I do not say it is bad to try to be rich. It is marvellous, wonderful. Why, what does it show? It shows that one can have the same amount of energy and struggle for freedom as one has for money. We know we have to give up money and all other things when we die, and yet, see the amount of energy we can put forth for them. But we, the same human beings, should we not put forth a thousandfold more strength and energy to acquire that which never fades, but which remains to us for ever? For this is the one great friend, our own good deeds, our own spiritual excellence, that follows us beyond the grave. Everything else is left behind here with the body.

That is the one great first step — the real desire for the ideal. Everything comes easy after that. That the Indian mind found out; there, in India, men go to any length to find truth. But here, in the West, the difficulty is that everything is made so easy. It is not truth, but development, that is the great aim. The struggle is the great lesson. Mind you, the great benefit in this life is struggle. It is through that we pass. If there is any road to Heaven, it is through Hell. Through Hell to Heaven is always the way. When the soul has wrestled with circumstance and has met death, a thousand times death on the way, but nothing daunted has struggled forward again and again and yet again — then the soul comes out as a giant and laughs at the ideal he has been struggling for, because he finds how much greater is he than the ideal. I am the end, my own Self, and nothing else, for what is there to compare to me own Self? Can a bag of gold be the ideal of my Soul? Certainly not! My Soul is the highest ideal that I can have. Realising my own real nature is the one goal of my life.

There is nothing that is absolutely evil. The devil has a place here as well as God, else he would not be here. Just as I told you, it is through Hell that we pass to Heaven. Our mistakes have places here. Go on! Do not look back if you think you have done something that is not right. Now, do you believe you could be what you are today, had you not made those mistakes before? Bless your mistakes, then. They have been angels unawares. Blessed be torture! Blessed be happiness! Do not care what be your lot. Hold on to the ideal. March on! Do not look back upon little mistakes and things. In this battlefield of ours, the dust of mistakes must be raised. Those who are so thin-skinned that they cannot bear the dust, let them get out of the ranks.

So, then, this tremendous determination to struggle a hundredfold more determination than that which you put forth to gain anything which belongs to this life, is the first great preparation.

And then along with it, there must be meditation Meditation is the one thing. Meditate! The greatest thing is meditation. It is the nearest approach to spiritual life — the mind meditating. It is the one moment in our daily life that we are not at all material — the Soul thinking of Itself, free from all matter — this marvellous touch of the Soul!

The body is our enemy, and yet is our friend. Which of you can bear the sight of misery? And which of you cannot do so when you see it only as a painting? Because it is unreal, we do not identify ourselves with it, eve know it is only a painting; it cannot bless us, it cannot hurt us. The most terrible misery painted upon a piece of canvas, we may even enjoy; we praise the technique of the artist, we wonder at his marvellous genius, even though the scene he paints is most horrible. That is the secret; that non-attachment. Be the Witness.

No breathing, no physical training of Yoga, nothing is of any use until you reach to the idea, "I am the Witness." Say, when the tyrant hand is on your neck, "I am the Witness! I am the Witness!" Say, "I am the Spirit! Nothing external can touch me." When evil thoughts arise, repeat that, give that sledge-hammer blow on their heads, "I am the Spirit! I am the Witness, the Ever-Blessed! I have no reason to do, no reason to suffer, I have finished with everything, I am the Witness. I am in my picture gallery — this universe is my museum, I am looking at these successive paintings. They are all beautiful. Whether good or evil. I see the marvellous skill, but it is all one. Infinite flames of the Great Painter!" Really speaking, there is naught — neither volition, nor desire. He is all. He — She — the Mother, is playing, and we are like dolls, Her helpers in this play. Here, She puts one now in the garb of a beggar, another moment in the garb of a king, the next moment in the garb of a saint, and again in the garb of a devil. We are putting on different garbs to help the Mother Spirit in Her play.

When the baby is at play, she will not come even if called by her mother. But when she finishes her play, she will rush to her mother, and will have no play. So there come moments in our life, when we feel our play is finished, and we want to rush to the Mother. Then all our toil here will be of no value; men, women, and children — wealth, name, and fame, joys and glories of life — punishments and successes — will be no more, and the whole life will seem like a show. We shall see only the infinite rhythm going on, endless and purposeless, going we do not know where. Only this much shall we say; our play is done.

The Cosmos And The Self

Everything in nature rises from some fine seed-forms, becomes grosser and grosser, exists for a certain time, and again goes back to the original fine form. Our earth, for instance, has come out of a nebulous form which, becoming colder and colder, turned into this crystallised planet upon which we live, and in the future it will again go to pieces and return to its rudimentary nebulous form. This is happening in the universe, and has been through time immemorial. This is the whole history of man, the whole history of nature, the whole history of life.

Every evolution is preceded by an involution. The whole of the tree is present in the seed, its cause. The whole of the human being is present in that one protoplasm. The whole of this universe is present in the cosmic fine universe. Everything is present in its cause, in its fine form. This evolution, or gradual unfolding of grosser and grosser forms, is true, but each case has been preceded by an involution. The whole of this universe must have been involute before it came out, and has unfolded itself in all these various forms to be involved again once more. Take, for instance, the life of a little plant. We find two things that make the plant a unity by itself — its growth and development, its decay and death. These make one unity the plant life. So, taking that plant life as only one link in the chain of life, we may take the whole series as one life, beginning in the protoplasm and ending in the most perfect man. Man is one link, and the various beasts, the lower animals, and plants are other links. Now go back to the source, the finest particles from which they started, and take the whole series as but one life, and you will find that every evolution here is the evolution of something which existed previously.

Where it begins, there it ends. What is the end of this universe? Intelligence, is it not? The last to come in the order of creation, according to the evolutionists, was intelligence. That being so, it must be the cause, the beginning of creation also. At the beginning that intelligence remains involved, and in the end it gets evolved. The sum total of the intelligence displayed in the universe must therefore be the involved universal intelligence unfolding itself, and this universal intelligence is what we call God, from whom we come and to whom we return, as the scriptures say.

Call it by any other name, you cannot deny that in the beginning there is that infinite cosmic intelligence.

What makes a compound? A compound is that in which the causes have combined and become the effect. So these compound things can be only within the circle of the law of causation; so far as the rules of cause and effect go, so far can we have compounds and combinations. Beyond that it is impossible to talk of combinations, because no law holds good therein. Law holds good only in that universe which we see, feel, hear, imagine, dream, and beyond that we cannot place any idea of law. That is our universe which we sense or imagine, and we sense what is within our direct perception, and we imagine what is in our mind. What is beyond the body is beyond the senses, and what is beyond the mind is beyond the imagination, and therefore is beyond our universe, and therefore beyond the law of causation. The Self of man being beyond the law of causation is not a compound, is not the effect of any cause, and therefore is ever free and is the ruler of everything that is within law. Not being a compound, it will never die, because death means going back to the component parts, destruction means going back to the cause. Because it cannot die, it cannot live; for both life and death are modes of manifestation of the same thing. So the Soul is beyond life and death. You were never born, and you will never die. Birth and death belong to the body only.

The doctrine of monism holds that this universe is all that exists; gross or fine, it is all here; the effect and the cause are both here; the explanation is here. What is known as the particular is simply repetition in a minute form of the universal. We get our idea of the universe from the study of our own Souls, and what is true there also holds good in the outside universe. The ideas of heaven and all these various places, even if they be true, are in the universe. They altogether make this Unity. The first idea, therefore, is that of a Whole, a Unit, composed of various minute particles, and each one of us is a part, as it were, of this Unit. As manifested beings we appear separate, but as a reality we are one. The more we think ourselves separate from this Whole, the more miserable we become. So, Advaita is the basis of ethics.

Who Is A Real Guru?

A real Guru is one who is born from time to time as a repository of spiritual force which he transmits to future generations through successive links of Guru and Shishya (disciple). The current of this spirit-force changes its course from time to time, just as a mighty stream of water opens up a new channel and leaves the old one for good. Thus it is seen that old sects of religion grow lifeless in the course of time, and new sects arise with the fire of life in them. Men who are truly wise commit themselves to the mercy of that particular sect through which the current of life flows. Old forms of religion are like the skeletons of once mighty animals, preserved in museums. They should be regarded with the due honour. They cannot satisfy the true cravings of the soul for the Highest, just as a dead mango-tree cannot satisfy the cravings of a man for luscious mangoes.

The one thing necessary is to be stripped of our vanities — the sense that we possess any spiritual wisdom — and to surrender ourselves completely to the guidance of our Guru. The Guru only knows what will lead us towards perfection. We are quite blind to it. We do not know anything. This sort of humility will open the door of our heart for spiritual truths. Truth will never come into our minds so long as there will remain the faintest shadow of Ahamkâra (egotism). All of you should try to root out this devil from your heart. Complete self-surrender is the only way to spiritual illumination.

On Art

The secret of Greek Art is its imitation of nature even to the minutest details; whereas the secret of Indian Art is to represent the ideal. The energy of the Greek painter is spent in perhaps painting a piece of flesh, and he is so successful that a dog is deluded into taking it to be a real bit of meat and so goes to bite it. Now, what glory is there in merely imitating nature? Why not place an actual bit of flesh before the dog?

The Indian tendency, on the other hand, to represent the ideal, the supersensual, has become degraded into painting grotesque images. Now, true Art can be compared to a lily which springs from the ground, takes its nourishment from the ground, is in touch with the ground, and yet is quite high above it. So Art must be in touch with nature — and wherever that touch is gone, Art degenerates — yet it must be above nature.

Art is — representing the beautiful. There must be Art in everything.

The difference between architecture and building is that the former expresses an idea, while the latter is merely a structure built on economical principles. The value of matter depends solely on its capacities of expressing *ideas*.

The artistic faculty was highly developed in our Lord Shri Ramakrishna, and he used to say that without this faculty none can be truly spiritual.

On Language

Simplicity is the secret. My ideal of language is my Master's language, most colloquial and yet most expressive. It must express the thought which is intended to be conveyed.

The attempt to make the Bengali language perfect in so short a time will make it cut and dried. Properly speaking, it has no verbs. Michael Madhusudan Dutt attempted to remedy this in poetry. The greatest poet in Bengal was Kavikankana. The best prose in Sanskrit is Patanjali's *Mahâbhâshya*. There the language is vigorous. The language of *Hitopadesha* is not bad, but the language of *Kâdambari* is an example of degradation.

The Bengali language must be modelled not after the Sanskrit, but rather after the Pâli, which has a strong resemblance to it. In coining or translating technical terms in Bengali, one must, however, use all Sanskrit words for them, and an attempt should be made to coin new words. For this purpose, if a collection is made from a Sanskrit dictionary of all those technical terms, then it will help greatly the constitution of the Bengali language.

The Sannyasin

In explanation of the term Sannyâsin, the Swami in the course of one of his lectures in Boston said:

When a man has fulfilled the duties and obligations of that stage of life in which he is born, and his aspirations lead him to seek a spiritual life and to abandon altogether the worldly pursuits of possession, fame, or power, when, by the growth of insight into the nature of the world, he sees its impermanence, its strife, its misery, and the paltry nature of its prizes, and turns away from all these — then he seeks the True, the Eternal Love, the Refuge. He makes complete renunciation (Sannyâsa) of all worldly position, property, and name, and wanders forth into the world to live a life of self-sacrifice and to persistently seek spiritual knowledge, striving to excel in love and compassion and to acquire lasting insight. Gaining these pearls of wisdom by years of meditation, discipline, and inquiry, he in his turn becomes a teacher and hands on to disciples, lay or professed, who may seek them from him, all that he can of wisdom and beneficence.

A Sannyasin cannot belong to any religion, for his is a life of independent thought, which draws from all religions; his is a life of realisation, not merely of theory or belief, much less of dogma.

The Sannyasin And The Householder

The men of the world should have no voice in the affairs of the Sannyâsins. The Sannyasin should have nothing to do with the rich, his duty is with the poor. He should treat the poor with loving care and serve them joyfully with all his might. To pay respects to the rich and hang on them for support has been the bane of all the Sannyasin communities of our country. A true Sannyasin should scrupulously avoid that. Such conduct becomes a public woman rather than one who professes to have renounced the world. How should a man immersed in Kâma-Kânchana (lust and greed) become a devotee of one whose central ideal is the renunciation of Kama-Kanchana? Shri Ramakrishna wept and prayed to the Divine Mother to send him such a one to talk with as would not have in him the slightest tinge of Kama-Kanchana; for he would say, "My lips burn when I talk with the worldly-minded." He also used to say that he could not even bear the touch of the worldly-minded and the impure. That King of Sannyasins (Shri Ramakrishna) can never be preached by men of the world. The latter can never be perfectly sincere; for he cannot but have some selfish motives to serve. If Bhagavân (God) incarnates Himself as a householder, I can never believe Him to be sincere. When a householder takes the position of the leader of a religious sect, he begins to serve his own interests in the name of principle, hiding the former in the garb of the latter, and the result is the sect becomes rotten to the core. All religious movements headed by householders have shared the same fate. Without renunciation religion can never stand.

Here Swamiji was asked — What are we Sannyasins to understand by renunciation of Kanchana (wealth)? He answered as follows:

With a view to certain ends we have to adopt certain means. These means vary according to the conditions of time, place, individual, etc.; but the end always remains unaltered. In the case of the Sannyasin, the end is the liberation of the Self and doing good to humanity — "आत्मनो मोक्षार्थं जगद्धिताय च"; and of the ways to attain it, the renunciation of Kama-Kanchana is the most important. Remember, renunciation consists in the total absence of all selfish motives and not in mere abstinence from external contact, such as avoiding to touch one's money kept with another at the same time enjoying all its benefits. Would that be renunciation? For accomplishing the two above-mentioned ends, the begging excursion would be a great help to a Sannyasin at a time when the householders strictly obeyed the injunctions of Manu and other law-givers, by setting apart every day a portion of their meal for ascetic guests. Nowadays things have changed considerably, especially, as in Bengal, where no Mâdhukari system prevails. Here it would be mere waste of energy to try to live on Madhukari, and you would profit nothing by it. The injunction of Bhikshâ (begging) is a means to serve the above two ends, which will not be served by that way now. It does not, therefore, go against the principle of renunciation under such circumstances if a Sannyasin provides for mere necessaries of life and devotes all his energy to the accomplishment of his ends for which he took Sannyasa. Attaching too much importance ignorantly to the means brings confusion. The end should never be lost sight of.

The Evils Of Adhikarivada

In one of his question classes the talk drifted on to the Adhikârivâda, or the doctrine of special rights and privileges, and Swamiji in pointing out vehemently the evils that have resulted from it spoke to the following effect:

With all my respects for the Rishis of yore, I cannot but denounce their method in instructing the people. They always enjoined upon them to do certain things but took care never to explain to them the reason for it. This method was pernicious to the very core; and instead of enabling men to attain the end, it laid upon their shoulders a mass of meaningless nonsense. Their excuse for keeping the end hidden from view was that the people could not have understood their real meaning even if they had presented it to them, not being worthy recipients. The Adhikarivada is the outcome of pure selfishness. They knew that by this enlightenment on their special subject they would lose their superior position of instructors to the people. Hence their endeavour to support this theory. If you consider a man too weak to receive these lessons, you should try the more to teach and educate him; you should give him the advantage of more teaching, instead of less, to train up his intellect, so as to enable him to comprehend the more subtle problems. These advocates of Adhikarivada ignored the tremendous fact of the infinite possibilities of the human soul. Every man is capable of receiving knowledge if it is imparted in his own language. A teacher who cannot convince others should weep on account of his own inability to teach the people in their own language, instead of cursing them and dooming them to live in ignorance and superstition, setting up the plea that the higher knowledge is not for them. Speak out the truth boldly, without any fear that it will puzzle the weak. Men are selfish; they do not want others to come up to the same level of their knowledge, for fear of losing their own privilege and prestige over others. Their contention is that the knowledge of the highest spiritual truths will bring about confusion in the understanding of the weak-minded men, and so the Shloka goes:

"न बुद्धिभेदं जनयेदज्ञानां कर्मसङ्गिनाम् ।
योजयेत्सर्वकर्माणि विद्वान् युक्तः समाचरन् ॥"

— "One should not unsettle the understanding of the ignorant, attached to action (by teaching them Jnâna): the wise man, himself steadily acting, should engage the ignorant in all work" (Gita, III. 26).

I cannot believe in the self-contradictory statement that light brings greater darkness. It is like losing life in the ocean of Sachchidânanda, in the ocean of Absolute Existence and Immortality. How absurd! Knowledge means freedom from the errors which ignorance leads to. Knowledge paving the way to error! Enlightenment leading to confusion! Is it possible? Men are not bold enough to speak out broad truths, for fear of losing the respect of the people. They try to make a compromise between the real, eternal truths and the nonsensical prejudices of the people, and thus set up the doctrine that Lokâchâras (customs of the people) and Deshâchâras (customs of the country) must be adhered to. No compromise! No whitewashing! No covering of corpses beneath flowers! Throw away such texts as, " तथापि लोकाचारः — Yet the customs of the people have to be followed." Nonsense! The result of this sort of compromise is that the grand truths are soon buried under heaps of rubbish, and the latter are eagerly held as real truths. Even the grand truths of the Gita, so boldly preached by Shri Krishna, received the gloss of compromise in the hands of future generations of disciples, and the result is that the grandest scripture of the world is now made to yield many things which lead men astray.

This attempt at compromise proceeds from arrant downright cowardice. Be bold! My children should be brave, above all. Not the least compromise on any account. Preach the highest truths broadcast. Do not fear losing your respect or causing unhappy friction. Rest assured that if you serve truth in spite of temptations to forsake it, you will attain a heavenly strength in the face of which men will quail to speak before you things which you do not believe to be true. People will be convinced of what you will say to them if you can strictly serve truth for fourteen years continually, without swerving from it. Thus you will confer the greatest blessing on the masses, unshackle their bandages, and uplift the whole nation.

On Bhakti-Yoga

The dualist thinks you cannot be moral unless you have a God with a rod in His hand, ready to punish you. How is that? Suppose a horse had to give us a lecture on morality, one of those very wretched cab-horses who move only with the whip, to which he has become accustomed. He begins to speak about human beings and says that they must be very immoral. Why? "Because I know they are not whipped regularly." The fear of the whip only makes one more immoral.

You all say there is a God and that He is an omnipresent Being. Close your eyes and think what He is. What do you find? Either you are thinking, in bringing the idea of omnipresence in your mind, of the sea, or the blue sky, or an expanse of meadow, or such things as you have seen in your life. If that is so, you do not mean anything by omnipresent God; it has no meaning at all to you. So with every other attribute of God. What idea have we of omnipotence or omniscience? We have none. Religion is realising, and I shall call you a worshipper of God when you have become able to realise the Idea. Before that it is the spelling of words and no more. It is this power of realisation that makes religion; no amount of doctrines or philosophies, or ethical books, that you may have stuffed into your brain, will matter much — only what you *are* and what you have *realised*.

The Personal God is the same Absolute looked at through the haze of Mâyâ. When we approach Him with the five senses, we can see Him only as the Personal God. The idea is that the Self cannot be objectified. How can the Knower know Itself ? But It can cast a shadow, as it were, if that can be called objectification. So the highest form of that shadow, that attempt at objectifying Itself, is the Personal God. The Self is the eternal subject, and we are struggling all the time to objectify that Self. And out of that struggle has come this phenomenal universe and what we call matter, and so on. But these are very weak attempts, and the highest objectification of the Self possible to us is the Personal God. This objectification is an attempt to reveal our own nature. According to the Sânkhya, nature is showing all these experiences to the soul, and when it has got real experience it will know its own nature. According to the Advaita Vedantist, the soul is struggling to reveal itself. After long struggle, it finds that the subject must always remain the subject; and then begins non-attachment, and it becomes free.

When a man has reached that perfect state, he is of the same nature as the Personal God. "I and my Father are one." He knows that he is one with Brahman, the Absolute, and projects himself as the Personal God does. He plays — as even the mightiest of kings may sometimes play with dolls.

Some imaginations help to break the bondage of the rest. The whole universe is imagination, but one set of imaginations will cure another set. Those that tell us that there is sin and sorrow and death in the world are terrible. But the other set — thou art holy, there is God, there is no pain — these are good, and help to break the bondage of the others. The highest imagination that can break all the links of the chain is that of the Personal God.

To go and say, "Lord, take care of this thing and give me that; Lord, I give you my little prayer and you give me this thing of daily necessity; Lord, cure my headache", and all that — these are not Bhakti. They are the lowest states of religion. They are the lowest form of Karma. If a man uses all his mental energy in seeking to satisfy his body and its wants, show me the difference between him and an animal. Bhakti is a higher thing higher than even desiring heaven. The idea of heaven is of a place of intensified enjoyment. How can that be God?

Only the fools rush after sense-enjoyments. It is easy to live in the senses. It is easier to run in the old groove, eating and drinking; but what these modern philosophers want to tell you is to take these comfortable ideas and put the stamp of religion on them. Such a doctrine is dangerous. Death lies in the senses. Life on the plane of the Spirit is the only life, life on any other plane is mere death; the whole of this life can be only described as a gymnasium. We must go beyond it to enjoy real life.

As long as *touch-me-not-ism* is your creed and the kitchen-pot your deity, you cannot rise spiritually. All the petty differences between religion and religion are mere word-struggles, nonsense. Everyone thinks, "This is my original idea", and wants to have things his own way. That is how struggles come.

In criticising another, we always foolishly take one especially brilliant point as the whole of our life and compare that with the dark ones in the life of another. Thus we make mistakes in judging individuals.

Through fanaticism and bigotry a religion can be propagated very quickly, no doubt, but the preaching of that religion is firm-based on solid ground, which gives everyone liberty to his opinions and thus uplifts him to a higher path, though this process is slow

First deluge the land (India) with spiritual ideas, then other ideas will follow The gift of spirituality and spiritual knowledge is the highest, for it saves from many and many a birth; the next gift is secular knowledge, as it opens the eyes of human beings towards that spiritual knowledge; the next is the saving of life; and the fourth is the gift of food.

Even if the body goes in practicing Sâdhanâs (austerities for realisation), let it go; what of that? Realisation will come in the fullness of time, by living constantly in the company of Sâdhus (holy men). A time comes when one understands that to serve a man even by preparing a Chhilam (earthen pipe) of tobacco is far greater than millions of meditations. He who can properly prepare a Chhilam of tobacco can also properly meditate.

Gods are nothing but highly developed dead men. We can get help from them.

Anyone and everyone cannot be an Âchârya (teacher of mankind); but many may become Mukta (liberated). The whole world seems like a dream to the liberated, but the Acharya has to take up his stand between the two states. He must have the knowledge that the world is true, or else why should he teach? Again, if he has not realised the world as a dream, then he is no better than an ordinary man, and what could he teach? The Guru has to bear the disciple's burden of sin; and that is the reason why diseases and other ailments appear even in the bodies of powerful Acharyas. But if he be imperfect, they attack his mind also, and he falls. So it is a difficult thing to be an Acharya.

It is easier to become a Jivanmukta (free in this very life) than to be an Acharya. For the former knows the world as a dream and has no concern with it; but an Acharya knows it as a dream and yet has to remain in it and work. It is not possible for everyone to be an Acharya. He is an Acharya through whom the divine power acts. The body in which one becomes an Acharya is very different from that of any other man. There is a science for keeping that body in a perfect state. His is the most delicate organism, very susceptible, capable of feeling intense joy and intense suffering. He is abnormal.

In every sphere of life we find that it is the person within that triumphs, and that personality is the secret of all success.

Nowhere is seen such sublime unfoldment of feeling as in Bhagavân Shri Krishna Chaitanya, the Prophet of Nadia.

Shri Ramakrishna is a force. You should not think that his doctrine is this or that. But he is a power, living even now in his disciples and working in the world. I saw him growing in his ideas. He is still growing. Shri Ramakrishna was both a Jivanmukta and an Acharya.

Ishvara And Brahman

In reply to a question as to the exact position of Ishvara in Vedantic Philosophy, the Swami Vivekananda, while in Europe, gave the following definition:

"Ishvara is the sum total of individuals, yet He is an Individual, as the human body is a unit, of which each cell is an individual. Samashti or collected equals God; Vyashti or analysed equals the Jiva. The existence of Ishvara, therefore, depends on that of Jiva, as the body on the cell, and vice versa. Thus, Jiva and Ishvara are coexistent beings; when one exists, the other must. Also, because, except on our earth, in all the higher spheres, the amount of good being vastly in excess of the amount of evil, the sum total (Ishvara) may be said to be all-good. Omnipotence and omniscience are obvious qualities and need no argument to prove from the very fact of totality. Brahman is beyond both these and is not a conditioned state; it is the only Unit not composed of many units, the principle which runs through all from a cell to God, without which nothing can exist; and whatever is real is that principle, or Brahman. When I think I am Brahman, I alone exist; so with others. Therefore, each one is the whole of that principle."

On Jnana-Yoga

All souls are playing, some consciously, some unconsciously. Religion is learning to play consciously.

The same law which holds good in our worldly life also holds good in our religious life and in the life of the cosmos. It is one, it is universal. It is not that religion is guided by one law and the world by another. The flesh and the devil are but degrees of difference from God Himself.

Theologians, philosophers, and scientists in the West are ransacking everything to get a proof that they live afterwards! What a storm in a tea-cup! There are much higher things to think of. What silly superstition is this, that you ever die! It requires no priests or spirits or ghosts to tell us that we shall not die. It is the most self-evident of all truths. No man can imagine his own annihilation. The idea of immortality is inherent in man.

Wherever there is life, with it there is death. Life is the shadow of death, and death, the shadow of life. The line of demarcation is too fine to determine, too difficult to grasp, and most difficult to hold on to.

I do not believe in eternal progress, that we are growing on ever and ever in a straight line. It is too nonsensical to believe. There is no motion in a straight line. A straight line infinitely projected becomes a circle. The force sent out will complete the circle and return to its starting place.

There is no progress in a straight line. Every soul moves in a circle, as it were, and will have to complete it; and no soul can go so low but that there will come a time when it will have to go upwards. It may start straight down, but it has to take the upward curve to complete the circuit. We are all projected from a common centre, which is God, and will come back after completing the circuit to the centre from which we started.

Each soul is a circle. The centre is where the body is, and the activity is manifested there. You are omnipresent, though you have the consciousness of being concentrated in only one point. That point has taken up particles of matter and formed them into a machine to express itself. That through which it expresses itself is called the body. You are everywhere. When one body or machine fails you, the centre moves on and takes up other particles of matter, finer or grosser, and works through them. Here is man. And what is God? God is a circle with circumference nowhere and centre everywhere.

Every point in that circle is living, conscious, active, and equally working. With our limited souls only one point is conscious, and that point moves forward and backward.

The soul is a circle whose circumference is nowhere (limitless), but whose centre is in some body. Death is but a change of centre. God is a circle whose circumference is nowhere, and whose centre is everywhere. When we can get out of the limited centre of body, we shall realise God, our true Self.

A tremendous stream is flowing towards the ocean, carrying little bits of paper and straw hither and thither on it. They may struggle to go back, but in the long run they; must flow down to the ocean. So you and I and all nature are like these little straws carried in mad currents towards that ocean of Life, Perfection, and God. We may struggle to go back, or float against the current and play all sorts of pranks, but in the long run we must go and join this great ocean of Life and Bliss.

Jnâna (knowledge) is "creedlessness"; but that does not mean that it despises creeds. It only means that a stage above and beyond creeds has been gained. The Jnâni (true philosopher) strives to destroy nothing but to help all. All rivers roll their waters into the sea and become one. So all creeds should lead to Jnana and become one. Jnana teaches that the world should be renounced but not on that account abandoned. To live in the world and not to be of it is the true test of renunciation.

I cannot see how it can be otherwise than that all knowledge is stored up in us from the beginning. If you and I are little waves in the ocean, then that ocean is the background.

There is really no difference between matter, mind, and Spirit. They are only different phases of experiencing the One. This very world is seen by the five senses as matter, by the very wicked as hell, by the good as heaven, and by the perfect as God.

We cannot bring it to sense demonstration that Brahman is the only real thing; but we can point out that this is the only conclusion that one can come to. For instance, there must be this oneness in everything, even in common things. There is the human generalisation, for example. We say that all the variety is created by name and form; yet when we want to grasp and separate it, it is nowhere. We can never see name or form or causes standing by themselves. So this phenomenon is Mâyâ — something which depends on the noumenon and apart from it has no existence. Take a wave in the ocean. That wave exists so long as that quantity of water remains in a wave form; but as soon as it goes down and becomes the ocean, the wave ceases to exist. But the whole mass of water does not depend so much on its form. The ocean remains, while the wave form becomes absolute zero.

The real is one. It is the mind which makes it appear as many. When we perceive the diversity, the unity has gone; and as soon as we perceive the unity, the diversity has vanished. Just as in everyday life, when you perceive the unity, you do not perceive the diversity. At the beginning you start with unity. It is a curious fact that a Chinaman will not know the difference in appearance between one American and another; and you will not know the difference between different Chinamen.

It can be shown that it is the mind which makes things knowable. It is only things which have certain peculiarities that bring themselves within the range of the known and knowable. That which has no qualities is unknowable. For instance, there is some external world, X, unknown and unknowable. When I look at it, it is X plus mind. When I want to know the world, my mind contributes three quarters of it. The internal world is Y plus mind, and the external world X plus mind. All differentiation in either the external or internal world is created by the mind, and that which exists is unknown and unknowable. It is beyond the range of knowledge, and that which is beyond the range of knowledge can have no differentiation. Therefore this X outside is the same as the Y inside, and therefore the real is one.

God does not reason. Why should you reason if you know? It is a sign of weakness that we have to go on crawling like worms to get a few facts, and then the whole thing tumbles down again. The Spirit is reflected in mind and in everything. It is the light of the Spirit that makes the mind sentient. Everything is an expression of the Spirit; the minds are so many mirrors. What you call love, fear, hatred, virtue, and vice are all reflections of the Spirit. When the reflector is base, the reflection is bad.

The real Existence is without manifestation. We cannot conceive It, because we should have to conceive through the mind, which is itself a manifestation. Its glory is that It is inconceivable. We must remember that in life the lowest and highest vibrations of light we do not see, but they are the opposite poles of existence. There are certain things which we do not know now, but which we can know. It is due to our ignorance that we do not know them. There are certain things which we can never know, because they are much higher than the highest vibrations of knowledge. But we are the Eternal all the time, although we cannot know it. Knowledge will be impossible there. The very fact of the limitations of the conception is the basis for its existence. For instance, there is nothing so certain in me as my Self; and yet I can only conceive of it as a body and mind, as happy or unhappy, as a man or a woman. At the same time, I try to conceive of it as it really is and find that there is no other way of doing it but by dragging it down; yet I am sure of that reality. "No one, O beloved, loves the husband for the husband's sake, but because the Self is there. It is in and through the Self that she loves the husband. No one, O beloved, loves the wife for the wife's sake, but in and through the Self." And that Reality is the only thing we know, because in and through It we know everything else; and yet we cannot conceive of It. How can we know the Knower? If we knew It, It would not be the knower, but the known; It would be objectified.

The man of highest realisation exclaims, "I am the King of kings; there is no king higher than I, I am the God of gods; there is no God higher than II I alone exist, One without a second." This monistic idea of the Vedanta seems to many, of course, very terrible, but that is on account of superstition.

We are the Self, eternally at rest and at peace. We must not weep; there is no weeping for the Soul. We in our imagination think that God is weeping on His throne out of sympathy. Such a God would not be worth attaining. Why should God weep at all? To weep is a sign of weakness, of bondage.

Seek the Highest, always the Highest, for in the Highest is eternal bliss. If I am to hunt, I will hunt the lion. If I am to rob, I will rob the treasury of the king. Seek the Highest.

Oh, One that cannot be confined or described! One that can be perceived in our heart of hearts! One beyond all compare, beyond limit, unchangeable like the blue sky! Oh, learn the All, holy one I Seek for nothing else!

Where changes of nature cannot reach, thought beyond all thought, Unchangeable, Immovable; whom all books declare, all sages worship; Oh, holy one, seek for nothing else!

Beyond compare, Infinite Oneness! No comparison is possible. Water above, water below, water on the right, water on the left; no wave on that water, no ripple, all silence; all eternal bliss. Such will come to thy heart. Seek for nothing else!

Why weepest thou, brother? There is neither death nor disease for thee. Why weepest thou, brother? There is neither misery nor misfortune for thee. Why weepest thou, brother? Neither change nor death was predicated of thee. Thou art Existence Absolute.

I know what God is — I cannot speak Him to you. I know not what God is — how can I speak Him to you? But seest thou not, my brother, that thou art He, thou art; He? Why go seeking God here and there? Seek not, and that is God. Be your own Self.

Thou art Our Father, our Mother, our dear Friend. Thou bearest the burden of the world. Help us to bear the burden of our lives. Thou art our Friend, our Lover, our Husband, Thou art ourselves!

The Cause Of Illusion

The question — what is the cause of Mâyâ (illusion)? — has been asked for the last three thousand years; and the only answer is: when the world is able to formulate a logical question, we shall answer it. The question is contradictory. Our position is that the Absolute has become this relative only apparently, that the Unconditioned has become the conditioned only in Maya. By the very admission of the Unconditioned, we admit that the Absolute cannot be acted upon by anything else. It is uncaused, which means that nothing outside Itself can act upon It. First of all, if It is unconditioned, It cannot have been acted upon by anything else. In the Unconditioned there cannot be time, space, or causation. That granted your question will be: "What caused that which cannot be caused by anything to be changed into this?" Your question is only possible in the conditioned. But you take it out of the conditioned, and want to ask it in the Unconditioned. Only when the Unconditioned becomes conditioned, and space, time, and causation come in, can the question be asked. We can only say ignorance makes the illusion. The question is impossible. Nothing can have worked on the Absolute. There was no cause. Not that we do not know, or that we are ignorant; but It is above knowledge, and cannot be brought down to the plane of knowledge. We can use the words, "I do not know" in two senses. In one way, they mean that we are lower than knowledge, and in the other way, that the thing is above knowledge. The X-rays have become known now. The very causes of these are disputed, but we are sure that we shall know them. Here we can say we do not know about the X-rays. But about the Absolute we cannot know. In the case of the X-rays we do not know, although they are within the range of knowledge; only we do not know them yet. But, in the other case, It is so much beyond knowledge that It ceases to be a matter of knowing. "By what means can the Knower be known?" You are always yourself and cannot objectify yourself. This was one of the arguments used by our philosophers to prove immortality. If I try to think I am lying dead, what have I to imagine? That I am standing and looking down at myself, at some dead body. So that I cannot objectify myself.

Evolution

(Some of the topics which precede and follow are taken from the answers given by the Swami to questions at afternoon talks with Harvard students on March 22 and 24, 1896. There have also been added notes and selections from unpublished lectures and discourses.)

In the matter of the projection of Akâsha and Prâna into manifested form and the return to fine state, there is a good deal of similarity between Indian thought and modern science. The moderns have their evolution, and so have the Yogis. But I think that the Yogis' explanation of evolution is the better one. "The change of one species into another is attained by the infilling of nature." The basic idea is that we are changing from one species to another, and that man is the highest species. Patanjali explains this "infilling of nature" by the simile of peasants irrigating fields. Our education and progression simply mean taking away the obstacles, and by its own nature the divinity will manifest itself. This does away with all the struggle for existence. The miserable experiences of life are simply in the way, and can be eliminated entirely. They are not necessary for evolution. Even if they did not exist, we should progress. It is in the very nature of things to manifest themselves. The momentum is not from outside, but comes from inside. Each soul is the sum total of the universal experiences already coiled up there; and of all these experiences, only those will come out which find suitable circumstances.

So the external things can only give us the environments. These competitions and struggles and evils that we see are not the effect of the involution or the cause, but they are in the way. If they did not exist, still man would go on and evolve as God, because it is the very nature of that God to come out and manifest Himself. To my mind this seems very hopeful, instead of that horrible idea of competition. The more I study history, the more I find that idea to be wrong. Some say that if man did not fight with man, he would not progress. I also used to think so; but I find now that every war has thrown back human progress by fifty years instead of hurrying it forwards. The day will come when men will study history from a different light and find that competition is neither the cause nor the effect, simply a thing on the way, not necessary to evolution at all.

The theory of Patanjali is the only theory I think a rational man can accept. How much evil the modern system causes! Every wicked man has a licence to be wicked under it. I have seen in this country (America) physicists who say that all criminals ought to be exterminated and that that is the only way in which criminality can be eliminated from society. These environments can hinder, but they are not necessary to progress. The most horrible thing about competition is that one may conquer the environments, but that where one may conquer, thousands are crowded out. So it is evil at best. That cannot be good which helps only one and hinders the majority. Patanjali says that these struggles remain only through our ignorance, and are not necessary, and are not part of the evolution of man. It is just our impatience which creates them. We have not the patience to go and work our way out. For instance, there is a fire in a theatre, and only a few escape. The rest in trying to rush out crush one another down. That crush was not necessary for the salvation of the building nor of the two or three who escaped. If all had gone out slowly, not one would have been hurt. That is the case in life. The doors are open for us, and we can all get out without the competition and struggle; and yet we struggle. The struggle we create through our own ignorance, through impatience; we are in too great a hurry. The highest manifestation of strength is to keep ourselves calm and on our own feet.

Buddhism And Vedanta

The Vedanta philosophy is the foundation of Buddhism and everything else in India; but what we call the Advaita philosophy of the modern school has a great many conclusions of the Buddhists. Of course, the Hindus will not admit that — that is the orthodox Hindus, because to them the Buddhists are heretics. But there is a conscious attempt to stretch out the whole doctrine to include the heretics also.

The Vedanta has no quarrel with Buddhism. The idea of the Vedanta is to harmonise all. With the Northern Buddhists we have no quarrel at all. But the Burmese and Siamese and all the Southern Buddhists say that there is a phenomenal world, and ask what right we have to create a noumenal world behind this. The answer of the Vedanta is that this is a false statement. The Vedanta never contended that there was a noumenal and a phenomenal world. There is one. Seen through the senses it is phenomenal, but it is really the noumenal all the time. The man who sees the rope does not see the snake. It is either the rope or the snake, but never the two. So the Buddhistic statement of our position, that we believe there are two worlds, is entirely false. They have the right to say it is the phenomenal if they like, but no right to contend that other men have not the right to say it is the noumenal.

Buddhism does not want to have anything except phenomena. In phenomena alone is desire. It is desire that is creating all this. Modern Vedantists do not hold this at all. We say there is something which has become the will. Will is a manufactured something, a compound, not a "simple". There cannot be any will without an external object. We see that the very position that will created this universe is impossible. How could it? Have you ever known will without external stimulus? Desire cannot arise without stimulus, or in modern philosophic language, of nerve stimulus. Will is a sort of reaction of the brain, what the Sânkhya philosophers call Buddhi. This reaction must be preceded by action, and action presupposes an external universe. When there is no external universe, naturally there will be no will; and yet, according to your theory, it is will that created the universe. Who creates the will? Will is coexistent with the universe. Will is one phenomenon caused by the same impulse which created the universe. But philosophy must not stop there. Will is entirely personal; therefore we cannot go with Schopenhauer at all. Will is a compound — a mixture of the internal and the external. Suppose a man were born without any senses, he would have no will at all. Will requires something from outside, and the brain will get some energy from inside; therefore will is a compound, as much a compound as the wall or anything else. We do not agree with the will-theory of these German philosophers at all. Will itself is phenomenal and cannot be the Absolute. It is one of the many projections. There is something which is not will, but is manifesting itself as will. That I can understand. But that will is manifesting itself as everything else, I do not understand, seeing that we cannot have any conception of will, as separate from the universe. When that something which is freedom becomes will, it is caused by time, space, and causation. Take Kant's analysis. Will is within time, space, and causation. Then how can it be the Absolute? One cannot will without willing in time.

If we can stop all thought, then we know that we are beyond thought. We come to this by negation. When every phenomenon has been negatived, whatever remains, that is It. That cannot be expressed, cannot be manifested, because the manifestation will be, again, will.

On The Vedanta Philosophy

The Vedantist says that a man is neither born nor dies nor goes to heaven, and that reincarnation is really a myth with regard to the soul. The example is given of a book being turned over. It is the book that evolves, not the man. Every soul is omnipresent, so where can it come or go? These births and deaths are changes in nature which we are mistaking for changes in us.

Reincarnation is the evolution of nature and the manifestation of the God within.

The Vedanta says that each life is built upon the past, and that when we can look back over the whole past we are free. The desire to be free will take the form of a religious disposition from childhood. A few years will, as it were, make all truth clear to one. After leaving this life, and while waiting for the next, a man is still in the phenomenal.

We would describe the soul in these words: This soul the sword cannot cut, nor the spear pierce; the fire cannot burn nor water melt it; indestructible, omnipresent is this soul. Therefore weep not for it.

If it has been very bad, we believe that it will become good in the time to come. The fundamental principle is that there is eternal freedom for every one. Every one must come to it. We have to struggle, impelled by our desire to be free. Every other desire but that to be free is illusive. Every good action, the Vedantist says, is a manifestation of that freedom.

I do not believe that there will come a time when all the evil in the world will vanish. How could that be? This stream goes on. Masses of water go out at one end, but masses are coming in at the other end.

The Vedanta says that you are pure and perfect, and that there is a state beyond good and evil, and that is your own nature. It is higher even than good. Good is only a lesser differentiation than evil.

We have no theory of evil. We call it ignorance.

So far as it goes, all dealing with other people, all ethics, is in the phenomenal world. As a most complete statement of truth, we would not think of applying such things as ignorance to God. Of Him we say that He is Existence, Knowledge, and Bliss Absolute. Every effort of thought and speech will make the Absolute phenomenal and break Its character.

There is one thing to be remembered: that the assertion — I am God — cannot be made with regard to the sense-world. If you say in the sense-world that you are God, what is to prevent your doing wrong? So the affirmation of your divinity applies only to the noumenal. If I am God, I am beyond the tendencies of the senses and will not do evil. Morality of course is not the goal of man, but the means through which this freedom is attained. The Vedanta says that Yoga is one way that makes men realise this divinity. The Vedanta says this is done by the realisation of the freedom within and that everything will give way to that. Morality and ethics will all range themselves in their proper places.

All the criticism against the Advaita philosophy can be summed up in this, that it does not conduce to sense-enjoyments; and we are glad to admit that.

The Vedanta system begins with tremendous pessimism, and ends with real optimism. We deny the sense-optimism but assert the real optimism of the Supersensuous. That real happiness is not in the senses but above the senses; and it is in every man. The sort of optimism which we see in the world is what will lead to ruin through the senses.

Abnegation has the greatest importance in our philosophy. Negation implies affirmation of the Real Self. The Vedanta is pessimistic so far as it negatives the world of the senses, but it is optimistic in its assertion of the real world.

The Vedanta recognises the reasoning power of man a good deal, although it says there is something higher than intellect; but the road lies through intellect.

We need reason to drive out all the old superstitions; and what remains is Vedantism. There is a beautiful Sanskrit poem in which the sage says to himself: "Why weepest thou, my friend? There is no fear nor death for thee. Why weepest thou? There is no misery for thee, for thou art like the infinite blue sky, unchangeable in thy nature. Clouds of all colours come before it, play for a moment, and pass away; it is the same sky. Thou hast only to drive away the clouds."

We have to open the gates and clear the way. The water will rush in and fill in by its own nature, because it is there already.

Man is a good deal conscious, partly unconscious, and there is a possibility of getting beyond consciousness. It is only when we become *men* that we can go beyond all reason. The words *higher* or *lower* can be used only in the phenomenal world. To say them of the noumenal world is simply contradictory, because there is no differentiation there. Man-manifestation is the highest in the phenomenal world. The Vedantist says he is higher than the Devas. The gods will all have to die and will become men again, and in the man-body alone they will become perfect.

It is true that we create a system, but we have to admit that it is not perfect, because the reality must be beyond all systems. We are ready to compare it with other systems and are ready to show that this is the only rational system that can be; but it is not perfect, because reason is not perfect. It is, however, the only possible rational system that the human mind can conceive.

It is true to a certain extent that a system must disseminate itself to be strong. No system has disseminated itself so much as the Vedanta. It is the personal contact that teaches even now. A mass of reading does not make men; those who were real men were made so by personal contact. It is true that there are very few of these real men, but they will increase. Yet you cannot believe that there will come a day when we shall all be philosophers. We do not believe that there will come a time when there will be all happiness and no unhappiness.

Now and then we know a moment of supreme bliss, when we ask nothing, give nothing, know nothing but bliss. Then it passes, and we again see the panorama of the universe moving before us; and we know that it is but a mosaic work set upon God, who is the background of all things.

The Vedanta teaches that Nirvâna can be attained here and now, that we do not have to wait for death to reach it. Nirvana is the realisation of the Self; and after having once known that, if only for an instant, never again can one be deluded by the mirage of personality. Having eyes, we must see the apparent, but all the time we know what it is; we have found out its true nature. It is the screen that hides the Self, which is unchanging. The screen opens, and we find the Self behind it. All change is in the screen. In the saint the screen is thin, and the reality can almost shine through. In the sinner the screen is thick, and we are liable to lose sight of the truth that the Atman is there, as well as behind the saint's screen. When the screen is wholly removed, we find it really never existed — that we were the Atman and nothing else, even the screen is forgotten.

The two phases of this distinction in life are — first, that the man who knows the real Self, will not be affected by anything; secondly, that that man alone can do good to the world. That man alone will have seen the real motive of doing good to others, because there is only one, it cannot be called egoistic, because that would be differentiation. It is the only selflessness. It is the perception of the universal, not of the individual. Every case of love and sympathy is an assertion of this universal. "Not I, but thou." Help another because you are in him and he is in you, is the philosophical way of putting it. The real Vedantist alone will give up his life for a fellow-man without any compunction, because he knows he will not die. As long as there is one insect left in the world, he is living; as long as one mouth eats, he eats. So he goes on doing good to others; and is never hindered by the modern ideas of caring for the body. When a man reaches this point of abnegation, he goes beyond the moral struggle, beyond everything. He sees in the most learned priest, in the cow, in the dog, in the most miserable places, neither the learned man, nor the cow, nor the dog, nor the miserable place, but the same divinity manifesting itself in them all. He alone is the happy man; and the man who has acquired that sameness has, even in this life, conquered all existence. God is pure; therefore such a man is said to be living in God. Jesus says, "Before Abraham was, I am." That means that Jesus and others like him are free spirits; and Jesus of Nazareth took human form, not by the compulsion of his past actions, but just to do good to mankind. It is not that when a man becomes free, he will stop and become a dead lump; but he will be more active than any other being, because every other being acts only under compulsion, he alone through freedom.

If we are inseparable from God, have we no individuality? Oh, yes: that is God. Our individuality is God. This is not the individuality you have now; you are coming towards that. Individuality means what cannot be divided. How can you call this individuality? One hour you are thinking one way, and the next hour another way, and two hours after, another way. Individuality is that which changes not — is beyond all things, changeless. It would be tremendously dangerous for this state to remain in eternity, because then the thief would always remain a thief and the blackguard a blackguard. If a baby died, he would have to remain a baby. The real individuality is that which never changes and will never change; and that is the God within us.

Vedantism is an expansive ocean on the surface of which a man-of-war could be near a catamaran. So in the Vedantic ocean a real Yogi can be by the side of an idolater or even an atheist. What is more, in the Vedantic ocean, the Hindu, Mohammedan, Christian, and Parsee are all one, all children of the Almighty God.

Law And Freedom

The struggle never had meaning for the man who is free. But for us it has a meaning, because it is name-and-form that creates the world.

We have a place for struggle in the Vedanta, but not for fear. All fears will vanish when you begin to assert your own nature. If you think that you are bound, bound you will remain. If you think you are free, free you will be.

That sort of freedom which we can feel when we are yet in the phenomenal is a glimpse of the real but not yet the real.

I disagree with the idea that freedom is obedience to the laws of nature. I do not understand what it means. According to the history of human progress, it is disobedience to nature that has constituted that progress. It may be said that the conquest of lower laws was through the higher. But even there, the conquering mind was only trying to be free; and as soon as it found that the struggle was also through law, it wanted to conquer that also. So the ideal was freedom in every case. The trees never disobey law. I never saw a cow steal. An oyster never told a lie. Yet they are not greater than man. This life is a tremendous assertion of freedom; and this obedience to law, carried far enough, would make us simply matter — either in society, or in politics, or in religion. Too many laws are a sure sign of death. Wherever in any society there are too many laws, it is a sure sign that that society will soon die. If you study the characteristics of India, you will find that no nation possesses so many laws as the Hindus, and national death is the result. But the Hindus had one peculiar idea — they never made any doctrines or dogmas in religion; and the latter has had the greatest growth. Eternal law cannot be freedom, because to say that the eternal is inside law is to limit it.

There is no purpose in view with God, because if there were some purpose, He would be nothing better than a man. Why should He need any purpose? If He had any, He would be bound by it. There would be something besides Him which was greater. For instance, the carpet-weaver makes a piece of carpet. The idea was outside of him, something greater. Now where is the idea to which God would adjust Himself? Just as the greatest emperors sometimes play with dolls, so He is playing with this nature; and what we call law is this. We call it law, because we can see only little bits which run smoothly. All our ideas of law are within the little bit. It is nonsense to say that law is infinite, that throughout all time stones will fall. If all reason be based upon experience, who was there to see if stones fell five millions of years ago? So law is not constitutional in man. It is a scientific assertion as to man that where we begin, there we end. As a matter of fact, we get gradually outside of law, until we get out altogether, but with the added experience of a whole life. In God and freedom we began, and freedom and God will be the end. These laws are in the middle state through which we have to pass. Our Vedanta is the assertion of freedom always. The very idea of law will frighten the Vedantist; and eternal law is a very dreadful thing for him, because there would be no escape. If there is to be an eternal law binding him all the time, where is the difference between him and a blade of grass? We do not believe in that abstract idea of law.

We say that it is freedom that we are to seek, and that that freedom is God. It is the same happiness as in everything else; but when man seeks it in something which is finite, he gets only a spark of it. The thief when he steals gets the same happiness as the man who finds it in God; but the thief gets only a little spark with a mass of misery. The real happiness is God. Love is God, freedom is God; and everything that is bondage is not God.

Man has freedom already, but he will have to discover it. He has it, but every moment forgets it. That discovering, consciously or unconsciously, is the whole life of every one. But the difference between the sage and the ignorant man is that one does it consciously and the other unconsciously. Every one is struggling for freedom — from the atom to the star. The ignorant man is satisfied if he can get freedom within a certain limit — if he can get rid of the bondage of hunger or of being thirsty. But that sage feels that there is a stronger bondage which has to be thrown off. He would not consider the freedom of the Red Indian as freedom at all.

According to our philosophers, freedom is the goal. Knowledge cannot be the goal, because knowledge is a compound. It is a compound of power and freedom, and it is freedom alone that is desirable. That is what men struggle after. Simply the possession of power would not be knowledge. For instance, a scientist can send an electric shock to a distance of some miles; but nature can send it to an unlimited distance. Why do we not build statues to nature then? It is not law that we want but ability to break law. We want to be outlaws. If you are bound by laws, you will be a lump of clay. Whether you are beyond law or not is not the question; but the thought that we are beyond law — upon that is based the whole history of humanity. For instance, a man lives in a forest, and never has had any education or knowledge. He sees a stone falling down — a natural phenomenon happening — and he thinks it is freedom. He thinks it has a soul, and the central idea in that is freedom. But as soon as he knows that it must fall, he calls it nature — dead, mechanical action. I may or may not go into the street. In that is my glory as a man. If I am sure that I must go there, I give myself up and become a machine. Nature with its infinite power is only a machine; freedom alone constitutes sentient life.

The Vedanta says that the idea of the man in the forest is the right one; his glimpse is right, but the explanation is wrong. He holds to this nature as freedom and not as governed by law. Only after all this human experience we will come back to think the same, but in a more philosophical sense. For instance, I want to go out into the street. I get the impulse of my will, and then I stop; and in the time that intervenes between the will and going into the street, I am working uniformly. Uniformity of action is what we call law. This uniformity of my actions, I find, is broken into very short periods, and so I do not call my actions under law. I work through freedom. I walk for five minutes; but before those five minutes of walking, which are uniform, there was the action of the will, which gave the impulse to walk. Therefore man says he is free, because all his actions can be cut up into small periods; and although there is sameness in the small periods, beyond the period there is not the same sameness. In this perception of non-uniformity is the idea of freedom. In nature we see only very large periods of uniformity; but the beginning and end must be free impulses. The impulse of freedom was given just at the beginning, and that has rolled on; but this, compared with our periods, is much longer. We find by analysis on philosophic grounds that we are not free. But there will remain this factor, this consciousness that I am free. What we have to explain is, how that comes. We will find that we have these two impulsions in us. Our reason tells us that all our actions are caused, and at the same time, with every impulse we are asserting our freedom. The solution of the Vedanta is that there is freedom inside — that the soul is really free — but that that soul's actions are percolating through body and mind, which are not free.

As soon as we react, we become slaves. A man blames me, and I immediately react in the form of anger. A little vibration which he created made me a slave. So we have to demonstrate our freedom. They alone are the sages who see in the highest, most learned man, or the lowest animal, or the worst and most wicked of mankind, neither a man nor a sage nor an animal, but the same God in all of them. Even in this life they have conquered relativity, and have taken a firm stand upon this equality. God is pure, the same to all. Therefore such a sage would be a living God. This is the goal towards which we are going; and every form of worship, every action of mankind, is a method of attaining to it. The man who wants money is striving for freedom — to get rid of the bondage of poverty. Every action of man is worship, because the idea is to attain to freedom, and all action, directly or indirectly, tends to that. Only, those actions that deter are to be avoided. The whole universe is worshipping, consciously or unconsciously; only it does not know that even while it is cursing, it is in another form worshipping the same God it is cursing, because those who are cursing are also struggling for freedom. They never think that in reacting from a thing they are making themselves slaves to it. It is hard to kick against the pricks.

If we could get rid of the belief in our limitations, it would be possible for us to do everything just now. It is only a question of time. If that is so, add power, and so diminish time. Remember the case of the professor who learnt the secret of the development of marble and who made marble in twelve years, while it took nature centuries.

The Goal And Methods Of Realisation

The greatest misfortune to befall the world would be if all mankind were to recognise and accept but one religion, one universal form of worship, one standard of morality. This would be the death-blow to all religious and spiritual progress. Instead of trying to hasten this disastrous event by inducing persons, through good or evil methods, to conform to our own highest ideal of truth, we ought rather to endeavour to remove all obstacles which prevent men from developing in accordance with their own highest ideals, and thus make their attempt vain to establish one universal religion.

The ultimate goal of all mankind, the aim and end of all religions, is but one — re-union with God, or, what amounts to the same, with the divinity which is every man's true nature. But while the aim is one, the method of attaining may vary with the different temperaments of men.

Both the goal and the methods employed for reaching it are called Yoga, a word derived from the same Sanskrit root as the English "yoke", meaning "to join", to join us to our reality, God. There are various such Yogas, or methods of union — but the chief ones are — Karma-Yoga, Bhakti-Yoga, Râja-Yoga, and Jnâna-Yoga.

Every man must develop according to his own nature. As every science has its methods, so has every religion. The methods of attaining the end of religion are called Yoga by us, and the different forms of Yoga that we teach, are adapted to the different natures and temperaments of men. We classify them in the following way, under four heads:

(1) Karma-Yoga — The manner in which a man realises his own divinity through works and duty.

(2) Bhakti-Yoga — The realisation of the divinity through devotion to, and love of, a Personal God.

(3) Raja-Yoga — The realisation of the divinity through the control of mind.

(4) Jnana-Yoga — The realisation of a man's own divinity through knowledge.

These are all different roads leading to the same centre — God. Indeed, the varieties of religious belief are an advantage, since all faiths are good, so far as they encourage man to lead a religious life. The more sects there are, the more opportunities there are for making successful appeals to the divine instinct in all men.

World-Wide Unity

Speaking of the world-wide unity, before the Oak Beach Christian Unity, Swami Vivekananda said:

All religions are, at the bottom, alike. This is so, although the Christian Church, like the Pharisee in the parable, thanks God that it alone is right and thinks that all other religions are wrong and in need of Christian light. Christianity must become tolerant before the world will be willing to unite with the Christian Church in a common charity. God has not left Himself without a witness in any heart, and men, especially men who follow Jesus Christ, should be willing to admit this. In fact, Jesus Christ was willing to admit every good man to the family of God. It is not the man who believes a certain something, but the man who does the will of the Father in heaven, who is right. On this basis — being right and doing right — the whole world can unite.

The Aim Of Raja-Yoga

Yoga has essentially to do with the meditative side of religion, rather than the ethical side, though, of necessity, a little of the latter has to be considered. Men and women are growing to desire more than mere revelation, so called. They want facts in their own consciousness. Only through experience can there be any reality in religion. Spiritual facts are to be gathered mostly from the superconscious state of mind. Let us put ourselves into the same condition as did those who claim to have had special experiences; then if we have similar experiences, they become facts for us. We can see all that another has seen; a thing that happened once can happen again, nay, *must*, under the same circumstances. Raja-Yoga teaches us how to reach the superconscious state. All the great religions recognise this state in some form; but in India, special attention is paid to this side of religion. In the beginning, some mechanical means may help us to acquire this state; but mechanical means alone can never accomplish much. Certain positions, certain modes of breathing, help to harmonise and concentrate the mind, but with these must go purity and strong desire for God, or realisation. The attempt to sit down and fix the mind on one idea and hold it there will prove to most people that there is some need for help to enable them to do this successfully. The mind has to be gradually and systematically brought under control. The will has to be strengthened by slow, continuous, and persevering drill. This is no child's play, no fad to be tried one day and discarded the next. It is a life's work; and the end to be attained is well worth all that it can cost us to reach it; being nothing less than the realisation of our absolute oneness with the Divine. Surely, with this end in view, and with the knowledge that we can certainly succeed, no price can be too great to pay.